THE
Archive Photographs
SERIES

HAZEL GROVE
AND
BRAMHALL

A postcard of Bramall Hall, Bramhall, from 1903.

THE
Archive Photographs
SERIES

HAZEL GROVE
AND
BRAMHALL

Compiled by
Heather Coutie

CHALFORD

The Chalford Publishing Company
St Mary's Mill, Chalford,
Stroud, Gloucestershire, GL6 8NX

ISBN 0 7524 0677 9

Typesetting and origination by
The Chalford Publishing Company
Printed in Great Britain by
Bailey Print, Dursley, Gloucestershire

The 50th anniversary celebrations of the Hazel Grove Industrial and Equitable Co-operative Society, 30 July 1910.

Contents

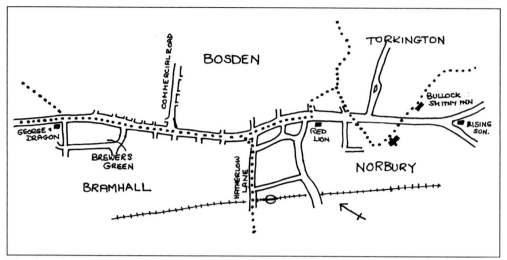

The dotted line on this map shows the meeting of the four manor boundaries along London Road, Hazel Grove.

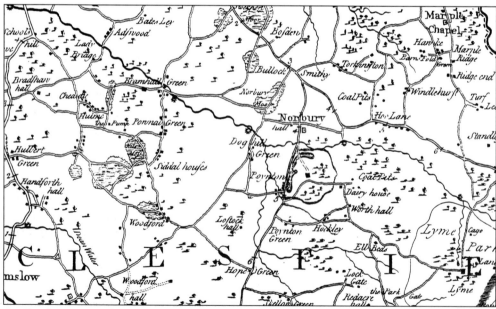

On Burdett's map of 1777 a number of the settlements mentioned in the book can be seen, including Kitts Moss near to Siddal Houses (Syddal), and Pownall Green. The halls at Handforth (owner of Bosden) and Lyme (later owner of Norbury) are also shown.

6

Introduction

A book of some 200 photographs of a community gives the opportunity to combine the two complementary objectives of pictorial nostalgia and local history. It is hoped that readers will enjoy looking at the photographs and seeing just how much places have changed over the years. The captions that accompany the photographs aim to present some of the history of the area and the interesting people who made it.

Although newcomers may well think of the villages of Hazel Grove and Bramhall as quite separate entities there are good reasons for combining them to form the geographical area covered by this book. Perhaps the most obvious one is that they have been combined for local government purposes for much of this century. In 1902 the Hazel Grove and Bramhall Urban District Council was formed, with offices at Torkington Lodge, and the two villages were linked in this way until both were incorporated into the Stockport Metropolitan Borough in 1974. Since many of the photographs in the book were taken during this period of time, it seems sensible to treat the two villages as a single entity.

There is a second, much older reason which goes back to the medieval manors. The area covered by the manor of Bramhall included much more than the present village of Bramhall, and extended as far as London Road in Hazel Grove. Its boundary followed the line of Hatherlow Lane and then north along the line of the A6 beyond Hazel Grove into parts of modern Davenport. So the distinction between what is Bramhall and what is Hazel Grove was nothing like as clear in the past as it may seem now, and in describing the history of the area through the captions to the photographs it is helpful to think of the two together.

In fact Hazel Grove was a nineteenth century creation and was originally called Bullock Smithy. Some time before 1560 a Richard Bullock was the tenant of a smithy here, which was working until 1819, and a Bullock Smithy Inn (pre 1624) stood nearby. One or the other gave its name to the settlement. The village grew along the road to the north and the boundaries of four of the local manors met along the line of the road, the present A6. These were Norbury, Torkington, Bosden in Handforth, known locally as Bosden, and of course Bramhall. The position of each can be seen on the map opposite. The Manchester to London turnpike (now the A6) was created in 1725 and passed through the centre of the village, and the road to Macclesfield was opened in 1762. By the turn of the nineteenth century Bullock Smithy had gained a reputation as 'an illiterate and disreputable place', possibly because of the drunkenness encouraged by the large number of inns built to serve the coach trade. Indeed, some of the passengers on the stage coaches begged them not to stop there, and the local dignitaries were ashamed to have their letters directed to such an infamous place. In 1836, in an effort to improve its reputation, the name of the village was changed to Hazel Grove with great pomp and pageantry.

Hazel Grove had two railway lines as well as the London Road, so transport played an important part in its industrial development. It became a centre for the textile industry and allied trades. The original cottage industries, like silk weaving and hatting, were augmented by the building of silk and cotton mills, and in this century engineering and various other industries have flourished. All this has naturally had an impact on housing.

By contrast, Bramhall started as a set of scattered hamlets round farms, like Syddal, Pownall Green and Bramhall Green, the last close to the hall. The manor remained under the control of the Davenports until 1877 when the last lord, John William Handley Davenport, sold the 1,918 acres of the manor to the Freeholders Company for £200,000. Much of the land was resold as going farms or as building plots and because of this Bramhall retained its agricultural base far longer than Hazel Grove. The concept of the present Bramhall village developed in the last century, probably after the station was opened in 1845, following which commuters were encouraged to live in the area close to the station. A by-product of grouping Hazel Grove and Bramhall together for the purposes of this book is that the two together provide a balanced cross section of life, one community developing its industry and the other retaining its farming roots.

While the book aims to present a wide variety of topics, it is clearly limited by the photographs available and cannot be claimed to be a comprehensive study of the area. Hopefully readers will find it both interesting and informative and will be tolerant about the inevitable gaps. Conforming with the sequence of the two villages in the name of the old Hazel Grove and Bramhall Urban District Council (hereafter abbreviated to UDC), Hazel Grove photographs usually come before Bramhall's in each of the sections.

One

Highways and Byways

The photographs in this section take the reader on a journey through Hazel Grove, with a glance at some of the roads off London Road (the A6), then across Bramhall Moor to the old settlement at Bramhall Green, and finally into the centre of modern Bramhall and the roads leading out on the other side.

The development of roads depends on a variety of influences. The highways or main roads were made to get from one centre to another, here the important one being the road to London, the present A6, which runs from one end of Hazel Grove village to the other. This divided at the Rising Sun Inn after the eighteenth century Macclesfield and Buxton turnpikes were opened to serve the developing stage coach trade.

Minor or byroads often followed the boundaries of the land and were to get from hamlet to hamlet, or farm to mill - there were two Mill Lanes, one for the Norbury Mill and the other for the Bramhall Mill. The old way from Bramhall to Stockport followed field boundaries and was not straightened out until Bramhall Lane South was developed. The roads between Bullock Smithy and Bramhall ran across manorial lands and were the responsibility of the inhabitants alongside them. Until the late eighteenth century occupiers of property here had to turn out 4-6 days a year to repair them. Carters from Bramhall had to pay a toll to the Leghs of Lyme to cross the Macclesfield highway in Norbury.

The most striking feature of the old photographs is the lack of traffic - how wonderful to be able to cycle down the centre of a road in safety!

Hazel Grove village begins at the northern end of London Road at the site of the old toll gate on the turnpike, and is seen here in 1910. The toll house was on the right but was demolished around 1890. To the left of the road is the manor of Bramhall and to the right, the manor of Bosden. The road to the left is Brewers Green. Opposite, in the far distance, was the Hazel Grove Silk Mill, known locally as the 'Top Shop' because it was at the top end of the village. The tram lines can be seen clearly. The humorous poem at the end of the book describes the Grovers as being so clean (or simple?) that they even black-leaded the tram lines.

Continuing southwards along London Road and looking north, also in 1910; on the right is the yard of the Bird in Hand Inn, which started as The Plough. It was a popular meeting place for many, from the Botanical Society to the pigeon fanciers, and the place where the Hazel Grove band practised. In the distance on the left is the imposing Co-operative Stores.

Leading from the centre of the village is Commercial Road, known as New Lane in 1749 but seen here in 1914. Several mills were built along the road, ending with the Wellington Mill in the valley. Near this were rows of cottages built for the employees including the attractive Brookfield Terrace, known as 'Long Row', with its twenty-three terraced cottages.

At this point on London Road the boundaries of three of the manors meet in the centre of the road. The Horse and Jockey on the right is in Bosden; The Grapes, nearest on the left, is in Norbury; and the Three Tuns beyond it is in Bramhall. It was once possible to stand in all three if you used a walking stick for your third 'leg', but this is not recommended in today's traffic.

The next stop is by the Mechanics Institute which is on the left, beyond the board of the Primitive Methodist Church. Opposite on the corner is J.T. Dean's new greengrocers shop and beside it one of the few surviving old cottages, the cobblers shop. This was owned by J. Ridgeway in the 1930s, which is the probable date of the photograph. The road still has its sets and tramlines.

Nearby is Chester Road, originally known as Button Lane, possibly after a bailiff to the Norbury estates who farmed the land alongside the road in the eighteenth century. In the distance, centre right, is the bridge over the railway line to Buxton. The buildings behind are the small factories on School Street.

Chester Road crossing the junction of Dean Lane and Jackson's Lane, c. 1900. Dean Lane has now been straightened to avoid the dog-leg junction. Chester Road still drops steeply into Mill Hill Hollow where the Ladybrook passes under the road through a very deep pool where, sadly, several adventurous children have been drowned in the past.

Returning to London Road, Charles Marsland stands before the weaving shed built by his uncle William behind his house in Marsland's Yard, when it was on the original line of London Road. At the beginning of the last century when the old road was straightened, William gained a new frontage on it and built three cottages for his relations.

The other end of the village, looking north from the Rising Sun Inn, c. 1910, at the junction of the London and Macclesfield Roads. The original Bullock Smithy was on the old road and would now be in the centre of the A6. It is around here that the boundaries between the Torkington and Norbury manors no longer follow the line of the road. (See the map on page 6)

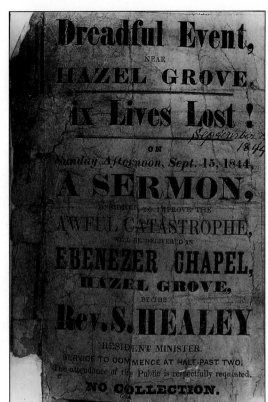

Dreadful Event,
NEAR
HAZEL GROVE.
ix Lives Lost!
ON
Sunday Afternoon, Sept. 15, 1844,
A SERMON,
DESIGNED TO IMPROVE THE
AWFUL CATASTROPHE,
WILL BE DELIVERED IN
EBENEZER CHAPEL,
HAZEL GROVE,
BY THE
Rev. S. HEALEY
RESIDENT MINISTER.
SERVICE TO COMMENCE AT HALF-PAST TWO.
The attendance of the Public is respectfully requested.
NO COLLECTION.

Torkington Road was the site of a tragedy. In September 1844 the stream which passes beneath the road from Torkington Lodge was blocked by debris after a cloudburst. The water built up against the retaining wall which collapsed, killing six operatives returning from the Wellington Mill and injuring sixteen others.

An unusual view of today's A6, or London Road, looking north towards the Rising Sun. It was taken at the turn of the century when the roads were not jammed with traffic and the horse provided a more leisurely form of transport. In the distance the tower of St Thomas's Church can be seen.

On the way to Bramhall these cottages on Mount Pleasant, Brewers Green, were demolished in 1987 when New Moor Road was built to replace the old narrow and twisting end of Bramhall Moor Lane. Brewers Green is shown on Ogilby's map of 1625 and was probably named after a Richard Brewer, who was there in 1589. A William Brewer, described as a fustian weaver, is recorded in the Bramhall court rolls of 1632.

Bramhall Moor Lane, originally Pepper Street, leads across the moor towards Bramhall. There were three other moors in the Bramhall manor - Kitts Moss, off Moss Lane, Doghill Moor, now under the Bramhall golf course, and Woodsmoor. The last was shared with Stockport and stretched across the A6 to the site of Stockport School. The cobbled lane, shown here in about 1910, has not a house in sight.

Bridge Lane, in 1901, from Bramhall Green. It was originally called Mill Lane since the Bramhall Mill was in the Ladybrook Valley. William Davenport owned the mill in the nineteenth century and it is said that after an argument with Mr Hampson, the miller, Davenport removed the roof and the mill fell into disrepair. The name change may have been to avoid confusion with another Mill Lane, further east, that led to the Norbury Mill.

The stocks originally stood near the gates to Bramall Hall on the Green, along with the pinfold. The latter was a small enclosure where the pinder kept straying stock until they were retrieved by their owner on payment of a fine. In the last century the stocks were no longer used to punish wrongdoers and fell into disrepair. They were restored as a feature and later re-erected in the courtyard of the hall.

Bridge Lane, Bramhall .

Bramhall Green, seen here in 1905, was the centre of the manor. The shop was owned by Mrs Simpson who advertised 'teas and hot water' for visitors to Bramall Park. At one time the Green had a blacksmith, a tailor, and an inn called the Shoulder of Mutton. Despite its caption, the photograph is taken from the bottom of Bridge Lane, looking up Bramhall Lane towards Stockport. Behind the lady in the trap - said to be the photographer's driver - is the bridge across the Ladybrook, which was built in the last century to replace the original ford.

From Bramhall Green the new drive on the right, built by Mr Nevill, leads up to the hall, where smoke comes from a chimney. The chapel extension was added by Nevill. The black and white stripes are painted on the bricks, which actually cover the timber framed wall beneath. The boy is standing, around 1900, at the present day entrance to the car park. The railings have long since gone.

Nearer to Bramhall, Robins Lane leaves Bramhall Lane South at Pownall Green. At the foot of the hill a cobbled track leads into the Carr Wood. Nearby is the crater of a landmine that fell in the Second World War, one of a stick which damaged the cottages at the top of the lane. The children are leaning against a broken gate and in front of them the road is paved with sets, which rattled cars until recently.

Still on Robins Lane, but now looking towards Pownall Green, this seventeenth century farmhouse has had many names including Ridgway's Tenement and Huxley's Tenement; today it is a private residence known as the Old Timbers. As a farm it had a dairy and originally, an outside flight of steps led up to the door in the gable end, above the shippen. (See page 42)

Bramhall Lane, Stockport.

Returning to Bramhall Lane South, some time before 1905, we find a pleasant tree-lined road with the sun shining on the parasols and one cyclist strolling down the centre of the road, still paved with sets, while another is riding on the footpath - possibly less bumpy?

Bramhall Lane, in bitter cold, looking north, c. 1898. Robert Rhodes is going for water at the pump in Benja Fold. In the centre distance it is just possible to make out the railway bridge by the station. On the left are the three houses known as 'The Villas', which Barbara Dean says were the first houses to be built on this part of Bramhall Lane in the middle of the last century.

These ladies are the six daughters of Mr Lander who was one of the first occupiers of one of the Bramhall Villas. Mrs Mary Leigh, daughter of Mr Linney who instigated the idea of a Bramhall Methodist Chapel, lived in one of the others. 'The Villas' have now been demolished.

Bramhall Lane South, *c.* 1904, the beginning of the modern village. On the right are the new shops built by William Adkinson in the 1890s, standing on the corner of Lumb Lane. On the opposite side of the road are some wooden huts, possibly used by Adkinson's men during the building of the new Methodist Chapel.

The so-called Roman road, which is marked on old maps, running south from the original end of Lumb Lane towards Woodford. Mr Earlam of Lumb Farm is said to have uncovered some Roman paving stones when he was digging holes for a gatepost. It was a pleasant footpath, known affectionately as 'Darling Shades'.

From the centre of the village looking north along Bramhall Lane towards Stockport, some time after 1905. The road is narrower than now and on the left is the Victoria Hotel. The early gas lamps were introduced in 1899 under an agreement with Stockport Corporation. It was in 1929 that the UDC proudly announced that electricity was provided to over half the potential consumers in Hazel Grove and Bramhall.

Woodford Road, Bramhall.

Again standing in the centre of Bramhall, this is an early view looking along Woodford Road. On the right is Cash's Smithy and beyond it the black and white timbers of Syddal Farm. Among the new shops on the left was a confectioners, built by a Mr Baxter, to be run by members of his family. In 1910 Mrs Agnes Stevens was there.

The Village, Bramhall.

T. W. Lofthouse, Photo, Manchester and Bramhall.

A third road out of the village is Ack Lane leading towards Cheadle Hulme, seen here *c.* 1910. Again the Victoria Hotel is in the picture to the right of the road. Before 1921 there were no shops beyond this, only houses, trees and hedges where the present Bramhall shopping precinct is built.

Another view of Ack Lane, at the turn of the century, looking towards the village from the Cheadle Hulme direction. Hardy's Farm is on the left and some of the newer houses line the road to the right. Ack Lane was also known as Hack Lane.

The last road from the centre of Bramhall is Moss Lane, shown looking towards the Victoria Hotel. It was named after the Kitts Moss which stretched away on the left of the road. Until the eighteenth century the 49 acres of the Moss were divided into strips, or moss rooms, about 30 metres wide, which were allocated to Bramhall tenants in the area to cut peat or run their livestock on. This was a common right on all the moors.

Some eighteenth and nineteenth century cottages on Moss Lane, built of brick with stone slab roofs. The nearest upstairs window has a horizontally sliding sash, an early form of sash window that is often found in period cottages. There were also eleven silk weavers' cottages on the lane.

The centre of the village looking towards Stockport, *c.* 1920s. Bramhall Lane is now wider and the old houses on the left are now modern shops. Opposite is a telephone box. Cars mix with the horse and cart and omnibus but it is still safe to cycle down the middle of the road.

Two

Halls and Houses

Bramall Hall, one of the most beautiful of Cheshire's black and white halls, has survived thanks to the restoration work of Charles Nevill and later, its purchase by the Hazel Grove and Bramhall UDC in 1935. Other manor houses were not so fortunate and became farmhouses. Torkington Hall is the second hall of that name, the first being on a moated site although no trace remains of the house within the moat. But it, like Norbury Hall and Bosden Hall, has seen the manorial lands disappear beneath modern development.

The area contains a number of interesting large houses, such as Brook House and Beech House in Hazel Grove, that belonged to gentry folk, while the coming of the railway to Bramhall attracted new people to the village to build grand houses such as Hillbrook Grange or the more modest 'Villas'.

The good agricultural land resulted in many farmhouses being built. Few of these remain as farms today because of the progressive urbanisation of the area but some of the older houses, such as Ridgway's Tenement in Bramhall, can trace their origins back to being farmhouses.

Farming continued later in Bramhall than Hazel Grove and the numerous leases and court roll references show that the tenants interchanged their farms more often than expected and were subject to the rules of the manor court. For example, in the early eighteenth century potato planting was restricted for fear it should exhaust the soil and marling was compulsory, which resulted in the digging of marl pits. These filled with water and in Bullock Smithy were a danger to inebriated revellers returning home across the fields in the dark.

Norbury Hall, near Five Ways, Hazel Grove. The manor of Norbury passed to the Hydes in the thirteenth century, who held it until the end of the seventeenth century when it was sold to the Leghs of Lyme. The first Norbury Hall, around 1577, was half timbered and badly decayed when this hall, of brick with stone quoins, was built alongside in the 1830s. Taken at Norbury Hall in about 1880, the people in the photograph are unknown.

Torkington Hall, Torkington Road. The timber framed hall may have been the home of John Torkenton, as his signature appears on the re-lease of Bullock Smithy to Richard Bullock in 1560. His ancestors had owned the manor from before 1200 until the middle of the fourteenth century when it was sold to the Leghs of Booths. The first Torkington Hall was a moated site on what is now Broadoak Farm.

Bramhall Manor, the Victorian home of Charles Heginbotham. In 1908 the Mirrlees Watson Company bought land alongside Bramhall Moor Lane to build a factory. Their sports club included football, cricket and golf and this house became the Ladies' Club House. On the now disused golf course evidence of the butts (raised platforms 2-3 metres wide) and reins (drainage channels between the butts) of eighteenth and nineteenth century farming can still be seen.

Beech House, Torkington Road, c. 1910. The lovely Georgian house and stables, on the right, were owned by John Gaskell Harrop in 1850. Beyond can be seen one of the two gatehouses to Torkington Lodge, built around 1790 by the Leghs of Booths. From the 1830s this was a girls' school until the 1860s, when Thomas Barlow bought it and built the gatehouses. His son, Sir John Emmott Barlow MP JP, sold the house to Hazel Grove and Bramhall UDC in 1937. The grounds are now Torkington Park.

Brook House, at the end of Bosden Fold Road, was the home of Charles Ireland and his sister. Some Grovers can remember him driving to the station in his pony and trap and the many grand carriages full of guests when the Irelands were entertaining. Local children were allowed into the garden to collect windfalls but were told 'not to step on the flower beds'. The house was photographed in the 1980s just before demolition.

This old timber framed cottage stood on the corner of Bramhall Park Road and Linney Road (originally Tenement Lane). It may date from the seventeenth century and was the Davenport's gamekeeper's cottage. In 1871 the gamekeeper was Samuel Hall. He would have been kept very busy as the rights to fish in the Ladybrook were jealously guarded and the stream was a great temptation to the local youth. The photograph was taken in about 1895.

Sir Thomas Rowbotham stands with his daughter Florence, and his niece Margaret Ainsworth, outside the billiard room of his home, Hillbrook Grange, in October 1939. He was an engineer and twice the Mayor of Stockport. He was also a staunch Methodist and a local philanthropist. On his death his daughter gave Hillbrook Grange, in memory of her parents, as a home for the elderly.

The old footbridge over Carr Brook, in Carr Wood. The wood was part of the Davenport estate but is now divided from the hall grounds by Carr Wood Road. Sir Thomas Rowbotham bought the wood to preserve it for the use of the public and it is still a haven, filled with wild flowers and bird song. It is known locally as the 'Fairy Wood', as it is said the fairies prevented the Davenports building their hall there.

Pownall Hall, *c.* 1916. In 1737 an inventory of William Pownall shows a six roomed house including a parlour and a 'best chamber', and goods valued at £403. The hall may have been altered or rebuilt in the last century. The earliest references to Pownalls in the village are in the fifteenth century. They were members of Dean Row Unitarian Chapel by the eighteenth century and friends of the Davenports of Bramall Hall.

The back of Pownall Hall just before its demolition in the 1960s. With 176 acres, the Pownalls were the largest land owners in Bramhall apart from the Davenports. They also owned land outside Bramhall. In 1858 the Pownall property passed from Peter Pownall to the sons of Sarah Brocklehurst. A book of local history, *The Diary of Peter Pownall, a Bramhall Farmer 1765-1858,* was published in 1989, edited by the author.

Among the cottages at Pownall Green are these on Bramhall Lane South. Sarah Pownall, Peter's sister, married John Brocklehurst of Macclesfield in 1783. He started at Acton & Street's, silk button manufacturers, then he set up a silk throwing firm and his sons, John and Thomas, became the largest silk cloth manufacturers in England. William, his eldest son, may have restored the cottages as they bear his initials and the date 1895.

The Brocklehursts sold off the farm stock and leased Pownall Hall. During the First World War George William Leech was there and he employed land-girls, two of whom are seen here - Molly Davies, later Williams (left) and Sally Taylor, later Neale. The girls, who were originally maids at the hall, are holding three of Leech's excellent horses. During the Second World War German prisoners of war worked on the farm.

The east front of Bramall Hall. This is Joseph Nash's romantic drawing of 1869, showing the hall in Elizabethan times with its long gallery, added by Sir William Davenport V. At that time a gatehouse wing enclosed the courtyard (demolished around 1774). Martha, wife of William X, inserted the sash windows that John Byng (later Viscount Torrington) referred to in his diary as 'lacking in taste', and removed the long gallery at the beginning of the nineteenth century.

The chapel of Bramall Hall. The chapel was described in the Torrington Diaries of 1794 as about to 'undergo repair' and as 'very low and ancient... the books are all fastened by chains'. The paintings on the west wall were covered in the late sixteenth century with the Ten Commandments. To the left of them is the original door to the chapel, which was closed by Charles Nevill in 1883 for a new staircase to the upper rooms.

The banqueting hall in the time of Charles Nevill. His father Thomas, who owned the Strines Printworks, bought the hall for Charles and his wife Mary in 1882. He spent many years in the sympathetic repair and restoration of the hall until his death in 1916. The tapestry covers the medieval wall paintings discovered by Nevill in 1887 when the walls were stripped of their plaster. He restored the room to its original appearance showing the roof trusses.

Bramhall Park looking across the artificial lakes. These were created by Charles Nevill by re-routing the Ladybrook so that there were trout for his favourite sport of fishing. His wife's letters make many references to fishing holidays. He also laid out the terraces. The trees in the foreground were still young in the 1950s and to the right of the hall stands the great tree that has now been felled.

The footbridge over the river in Bramhall Park at the beginning of the century. The path that goes diagonally across the grass in front of the hall is on the line of the original drive. This was diverted well away from the chapel wall to its present route in 1888 by Charles Nevill, to make it easier for the horses and to give extra privacy to the occupants of the hall.

Salusbury Pryce Humphries entered the Navy at the age of 12 in 1790 and rapidly rose to have his own command. He was made a scapegoat by the British Government over the Chesapeke incident of 1807. He left the Navy and in 1810 married Maria, the younger natural daughter of William Davenport X. In 1838 he inherited the manor through his wife. He led a distinguished life both locally and in the county, and died in 1845.

Bosden Hall Farm House, Bosden, in 1985. Bosden may come from Bossa's dun - the hill of Bossa. It was first recorded in 1232 when Henry de Honefort (Handforth) acquired the manor. Until this century it was part of the parish of Cheadle. The first timber framed hall became a barn when the new hall was built in the mid 1700s. Some of the original 94 acres were built on in 1919, and the rest was developed in 1935.

Hatherlow Farm. Now in Hazel Grove, the farm on Bramhall Moor was owned by the Davenports of Bramhall. In 1777 Thomas Grundy, the occupier, was fined at the manor court for not clearing his ditches. Around 1853 a Miss Beard had a day and boarding school here. Later Johnny Holland and his son-in-law, Thomas Moult, ran the farm and provided a twice daily milk delivery in the Grove. The house was demolished in 1969 and the land is now part of an industrial estate.

The original Norbury Farm was on Norbury Moor which lay between Chester Road, Jackson's Lane and Hatherlow Lane. The farm passed to the Leghs of Lyme when they purchased the manor of Norbury. In the 1850s the Grundys occupied the farm. Now the duck pond, farm and all the fields are a housing estate and only 'Moorfield' County Primary School preserves one of the field names.

Cow Lane, a continuation of Grosvenor Street, Hazel Grove, in 1901. The horse and cart is on its way to Old Fold Farm, originally called Locker's Fold after Joseph Locker, its occupant in the 1840s. It was 'rebuilt' according to a date stone 'PPB 1878', but its much older timber frame was revealed in the 1980s when the owner, Mr Hague, renovated the house. 'PPB' may refer to Peter Pownall Brocklehurst, the grandson of Sarah Brocklehurst.

Chip Hill Farm in Bramhall was on the boundary of Cheadle Hulme, on the south side of Moss Lane. It was occupied by Samuel Clarke in 1792. William Worthington bought the farm with its 9 Cheshire acres (similar to the modern hectare) in 1801 for £915. It remained in the family until the 1930s when, with Tan Pits Farm in Cheadle Hulme, another of their farms, it was sold for housing development.

Lumb Farm, shown here in the 1890s, was on the north side of the present Lumb Lane and was occupied around 1900 by William Adkinson, the farmer and builder, although Barbara Dean notes that he actually lived at Pownall Hall. He has many local buildings to his credit. In 1910 he was a member of the first Hazel Grove and Bramhall UDC. The farm was demolished and only a black and white cottage, which was a loom house, survives.

Hardy's Farm was on Ack Lane, Bramhall. In 1645 Margaret Hardy, a widow, farmed it. The Bramhall court rolls (1688-1732) frequently record offices held by Joshua Hardy. The date stone of 1745 probably referred to a renovation. In 1822 Robert Hardy and three of his sons died within 6 months of each other. Here (left to right) are Elia, Ada, Edith, Sidney, Frances and Joseph Holland, who farmed it in 1910. The farm was sold for building in about 1980.

Harvest time on Kitts Moss. The sheaves of corn have been left to dry in stooks before being pitchforked onto a wagon and taken to the farmyard. The Moss was originally moorland, but by the eighteenth century the peat was used up, so the quality of the land was improved for agriculture. Strips were sometimes exchanged between the owners, and Peter Pownall and Robert Hardy did this in 1785.

Clarke's Farm in 1895. Near to Bramall Hall, the farm had fields on either side of Bramhall Lane South. Indeed since the new road cut through them, the old road probably followed the field boundaries to the west. Randle Clarke was there in 1717 and Matthew Clarke is on the 1840 tithe map. Henry and Mary Clarke, brother and sister, continued the farm until 1914. It was demolished in about 1920.

This hay cart has overturned on its way along Bramhall Lane to Clarke's Farm. What chaos it would cause in today's traffic conditions!

This wintry picture shows the barn which was part of Clarke's Farm. It stands on the site of today's modern flats, looking down onto the roundabout at Bramhall Green. Mr Walter Simpson and his son are standing on the corner of the road that was to become Carr Wood Road.

Ridgway's Tenement on Robins Lane, Bramhall, has changed its name with its owners. In 1674 John Barrett was the farmer, but by 1710 it was Peter Ridgway's. In the 1720s Richard Huxley was the owner who passed it to his son Thomas in 1739, when it was known as Huxley's Tenement. The timber framed cruck cottage was altered when a box framed cross wing was added in the eighteenth century using one pair of crucks as beams. Another cruck is still in place. Later bricks covered the original black and white walls.

Syddal House in Bramhall in 1905. A Thomas Syddal was recorded here in 1598 and the family gave the name Syddal to the area. The Browne family, wealthy merchants, lived nearby. At the beginning of this century there were two 'Syddal' houses - one, Syddal Farm, was demolished in the 1920s to build Syddal Road and this one stood on the site of Woolworth's.

White Lodge (formerly Lodge Farm) overlooked Bramhall Green. It was given to Samuel Hunt Esq, husband of Anne, the elder natural daughter of William Davenport X, in 1806. It was leased by the Garners who specialised in dairy farming. The last William Garner was chairman of the first Hazel Grove and Bramhall UDC. In 1922 the 66 acres were sold and Broadway and nearby roads were built.

Wallbank Farm, near the top of Bridge Lane, was a Davenport jointure house, as was Lodge Farm. The widowed Dame Dorothy held it in 1632. The path beside it was once known as Pepper Street, the old road to Stockport from the Roman road on Lumb Lane. On the corner of Jackson's Lane was New Barns, a cruck framed farm house built around 1640 and demolished when the lane was widened in 1889. The old road continued across the fields to Woodsmoor and Stockport.

Harvesting was done in a more leisurely manner in 1903. Here an unknown local farmer guides his two great horses through a wheat field filled with wild flowers.

Three

Churches and
Education

From medieval times the people of three of the manors had to attend the parish church of St Mary's in Stockport, while those in Bosden went to St Mary's at Cheadle because it belonged to the manor of Handforth. In 1465 Hamnet Hyde of Norbury built a chapel of ease near the boundary of Norbury and Poynton. In 1672 the then curate, John Jollie, was removed for refusing to obey the Act of Uniformity, though he later returned. The chapel was refurbished by the Leghs of Lyme in about 1689, but by 1829 it was dilapidated and rarely attended. The nineteenth century saw the growth of non-conformist chapels in the area and with the new parish boundaries came St Thomas's of Norbury, which soon served all Hazel Grove; later St Michael's was built in Bramhall.

The earliest recorded 'Scoole Maister' was in Bramhall in 1588. In 1741 Warren Davenport built a charity school for the education of poor children on Bramhall Green. At Norbury in 1760 Peter Legh gave land (School Field) for a school to 'clothe and educate 12 poor children of Norbury'. Six were clothed by Squire Legh and six by 'Old Mr Heywood'. The local farmers built the school with a public subscription and two years later there were thirty pupils, eighteen of them paying fees. It was demolished around 1851.

Modern education in the area was the product of the rivalry between the churches and chapels. Early Sunday schools included reading and writing classes and the nineteenth century Education Acts increased the opportunities for new day schools. Many of those church schools have become modern local authority schools. Private education in the nineteenth century ranged from a small school in a barn in Benja Fold, Bramhall, to a ladies' seminary in the 1830s in Torkington Lodge, Hazel Grove, while at the Mechanics Institute there was a British School in 1871 and a High School in 1872.

Bullock Smithy Chapel, on Chapel Street, Hazel Grove. It was built by the Revd David Simpson in 1774 after he was discharged from St Michael's Church, Macclesfield, for his Wesleyan sympathies. At that time the parish church was St Mary's in Stockport. After Simpson left, the Methodists bought the chapel in 1784. In 1786 John Wesley preached there and had little good to say about the people of the village.

The Sunday school, Wesley Street. The first Wesleyan Sunday school in Hazel Grove was in a cottage in Torkington Lane in 1784. By 1816 it had moved to a room in Marsland's cotton mill on Engine Gennel, near Queens Road. There were 350 children on the roll, who were also taught to read and write. A new Sunday school was built in Chapel Street in 1823 for 400 scholars. By 1876 the building shown here had been enlarged to take 600 day school pupils.

In 1883 this new Wesleyan Methodist Church was built on the corner of Chapel and Wesley Streets at a cost of £6,000, on land given by Laurence Arden. A new Sunday school was built in 1914 within a few yards of the church, and opened with much celebration and music provided by the choir under Mr J. Worsley Harrop. This church was demolished in 1972 when the present church was built.

Chapel Street Public Elementary School. In 1902 the Education Act abolished the school boards and gave borough and county councils control over elementary education in both church and state schools. So in 1914, under the auspices of the Local Education Authority, a new school was built to replace the old Wesleyan school. It is still open and is now known as the Hazel Grove Junior School.

The United Methodist Free Church, or Christian Refuge, on the corner of Lever Street, was built in 1836 by the supporters of the Revd Dr Samuel Warren after he was refused entry to the Wesley Street Chapel in 1835 and preached in the churchyard. They left the chapel and met initially over the stable behind the Three Tuns. In 1877 a new church was built in Napier Street and the original refuge became the Sunday school.

The Mount Zion Chapel on Commercial Road was built in 1849 by the Primitive Methodists. When their new chapel was built on London Road in 1897, this chapel was sold to the Roman Catholics and opened as St Peter's Church. The New Mission Roman Catholic Church was opened in 1931, on Green Lane. The chapel was later owned by the Permanent Building Society, which became part of the Northern Rock Building Society, and was demolished in the 1980s.

The Christian Bethal was erected by the Independent Methodists in 1866. In 1956 the Elim Central Mission in Stockport purchased the building as the Full Gospel Tabernacle. In 1979 it was demolished to make way for New Moor Lane, and the Full Gospel Church was built 200 yards to the south. During site clearance an old well was found 'where women and children with their buckets and dandies (a tub on wheels) gossiped happily' according to Sam Penney.

The Primitive Methodist Church or London Road Chapel was built in 1897 next to the Civic Hall on School Field. It can be seen behind the crowd at the unveiling of the War Memorial when only the relatives of the dead were allowed within the railings. The church was closed in 1960 when it was amalgamated with the Wesley Street Methodist Church.

The Ebenezer Chapel (the first Congregational Church) was built in 1827 near the top of Commercial Road. It was the result of a mission started by Theophillus Davies in Bullock Smithy in 1823 when he preached to people in the backyard of his house, summoned by the town-crier. When the new chapel was built further down the road, this building became the Sunday school, with 350 scholars and 28 teachers.

John Benison, born in about 1810, was a local character and well known in the village. He was much loved by all the children who called him grandfather. Although he couldn't remember their names he could recognise all of them. He died aged 86, and was buried in the Ebenezer churchyard, when Thomas Penney played the *Dead March* on the organ as a mark of sympathy and respect.

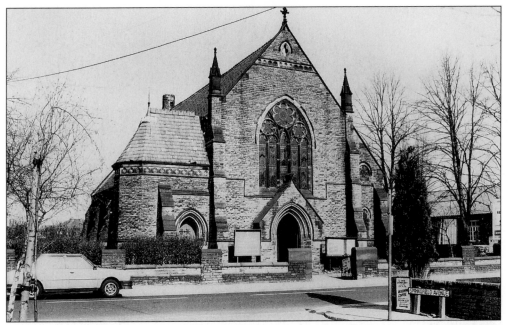

This is the second Congregational Chapel which was opened in 1883 at a cost of over £3,000. Recently this also was demolished and now a new church has been built on the site of the first chapel and churchyard. It is now known as the United Reformed Church after the union of the Congregational and Presbyterian churches.

St Thomas's Church, Norbury. It was built to replace the derelict Norbury Chapel on land given by Thomas Legh of Lyme and was financed by £2,000 from the Commissioners for Building New Churches, and donations from Peter Legh of Booths, the Vernons of Poynton, and other local people. It was consecrated in 1834. This view in 1890 shows the church across open fields.

The Norbury Church Girl Guides are seen here on parade to celebrate the dedication of the new bells and the new chancel by the Bishop of Chester on 24 October 1925. Four of the old bells were recast and four new bells were added at a cost of £680. Two of the oldest bells, dating from 1617, were hung in the west porch. Later the Girl Guides were given the task of cleaning the chancel and Friday night became 'chancel night'.

The 1st Norbury was the first Brownie pack in the Stockport area, having been formed over eighty years ago. In this 1947 photograph the Brown Owl in the centre is Margaret Briggs. On her left is the Pack Leader Joyce Robson (née Bradbury) and on her right is Tawny Owl Jean Norris (née Addison). The Boy Scouts were started in 1919.

Norbury National School was built in 1834 on ground beside St Thomas's Church. The site, and the materials from the demolished Bullock Smithy Chapel, were donated by Thomas Legh of Lyme. A public subscription and a grant from the National Society for the Education of the Poor in the Principles of the Established Church, paid for it. Later a house for the schoolmaster was built to the right of the school.

The school was ready to open in 1835 but due to lack of funds it started only as a Sunday school with some 100 scholars. It was not until 1840 that the money for an infant teacher was available, and later the school only survived because Mrs Wilkinson accepted a cut in her salary. In 1870, under Forster's Act, the school was extended and by 1902 had three departments. The headmaster, Mr Locket, is seen here with the children in 1904.

The Mechanics Institute was started by Mr Brookes, headmaster of Norbury School, in 1868 in a shop for 'the benefit of local mechanics and apprentices'. Mr David Clayton Shore gave the land and £300 and, with a public subscription, this building was opened on 19 April 1871. Voluntary teachers took evening classes and in 1881 recreation rooms were opened. Many local societies and two small private schools used the premises. The lady holding her baby is Mrs Maddocks.

Robert Joplin Fletcher. Apprenticed at Christy's Hatworks, he later opened his own works in Oak Street and then became an accountant. As an active Anglican he worked for both Sunday and day schools and the Mechanics Institute. He was an Independent on Hazel Grove and Bramhall UDC in 1901. His series of lectures on local history to the Hazel Grove Literary Society was published as *A Short History of Hazel Grove*. He died aged 83 on 23 October 1928.

The Baptist or 'Lamb' Chapel on Woodford Road, Bramhall - so called because it was opposite the Lamb Inn, which closed some time towards the end of the nineteenth century. As the Davenports were not in favour of non-conformist chapels it was built on the manor boundary, and was the first place of worship built in the village after the chapel at Bramall Hall. It was erected in 1856 and enlarged in 1888.

Ford's Lane, Bramhall, in the early 1900s. The roof of the Evangelical Church, erected in 1884, can just be seen beyond the gable on the left. George Geddes, an itinerant preacher, started the movement in a cottage on Benja Fold. A Mr John Porter built the church and his daughters started the Sunday school there. Some years later the congregation raised the money to buy the church. A new church was opened opposite in 1966, and the original is now a hall.

The Bramhall Methodist Church. In 1860 a group of four Methodists from Cheadle Hulme formed a Methodist Society in Thomas Hough's cottage on Pownall Green. In 1871 the first chapel, 'a plain brick building' seating 180 people, was opened with help from Sir Thomas Rowbotham. In 1904 William Adkinson built a new chapel, seen here in 1910, beside the old chapel which became the Sunday school.

St Michael and All Angels Church, Bramhall, shortly after it was built in 1910. In 1888 Revd Arthur Symonds, the Rector of St Thomas's Parish Church in Stockport, opened a mission in Bramhall, holding regular services on Sunday evenings at the Bramhall Board School on Bramhall Lane South. In 1890 a Mission Church of St Michael and All Angels was opened next to the school and was used until the new church was built. It is still standing.

Some workmen pause for a photograph during the building of Bramhall's new church, designed to meet the demands of a growing population. Funds were raised by a committee, land was bought and the foundation stone laid on 10 July 1909. It cost £5,213 to build and furnish. In January 1911 it became the new parish church of Bramhall. The tower and porch were added in 1963.

The first Congregational Church in Bramhall was built in 1904 on the corner of Robins Lane and was used as a combined church and Sunday school. The black and white building shown in the photograph, in about 1937, was built onto the church in 1928 as a church hall. A new church, known now as the United Reformed Church, was built at the beginning of this decade and the hall, described in the 1920s as a 'temporary structure', was replaced in 1996.

The Bramhall Board School, built by William Adkinson. This was opened on 2 July 1877 as a result of the 1870 Education Act's grants for new schools so that all children could go to school. It started with nineteen pupils and Robert Buckley as headmaster. In those days many children missed school to help with farm work. A new school was built opposite in the 1970s and the old school was demolished in 1996.

Pupils at Bramhall Grammar School, a fee-paying school, in 1912. The two masters in mortar boards, standing at the back, are the headmaster Mr Haylett (on the left) and Mr Williams. The headmaster used his clarinet to set the note for the hymn singing. The caps were the only school uniform. Later the building was the Bramhall Library, now rebuilt on the same site.

Four

Transport

The gradual change from horse and cart, to horse tram and the internal combustion engine, is shown in this selection of photographs. It starts with the blacksmiths who not only shoed the horses but were often farriers or 'horse doctors' as well. They were also called upon to make and repair farm machinery and tools. The last smithy in Hazel Grove only closed in the 1950s. Alongside them were the wheelwrights, highly skilled men in the making and mending of wagon wheels. Not surprisingly many such businesses, like Cash's Smithy in Bramhall, changed over to serving the new motor vehicles, both as garages and coach builders. The development of new forms of public transport is also illustrated, as the old stage coaches gave way to horse buses and the later electric trams.

But it was the railways that probably had the greatest influence of all. In Hazel Grove the railway provided a link for industry as attempts to open a canal in the eighteenth century had resulted in failure. Two lines crossed in Hazel Grove and two stations were built. The London & North Western Railway built the present one, in use today, in 1857, while the Midland Railway built one in 1902 for Sir John Barlow's use because he allowed them to lay their track across his land! This has been closed for many years. The railway came to Bramhall in 1845 as the Macclesfield Branch of the London & North Western Railway, and brought with it commuters and many new houses.

The horse was vital to both transport and the farm and Bramhall still had blacksmiths at the beginning of this century. This smithy was on Ford's Lane and was opened by James Ford, probably in the 1870s. Taken in about 1900, it shows John Ford, the smith and farrier, shoeing the horse of Mr Jessie Blunt (left) who is holding it. Elias Holland (right) waits with his horse *Britain*, and Joe Ford stands beside him.

The Ford family in the 1890s, with Mr and Mrs James Ford senior (sitting centre) and Mr and Mrs Joe Ford on either side. Behind stand the sons Walter, Arthur and John (seen above). John was known as a *raconteur* and was a great asset at parties. He also attended church regularly every Sunday but had a reputation for falling asleep.

The Bramhall Smithy was in the centre of the village. It was recorded in the 1841 census when James Cash, aged 50, was the blacksmith. His son Thomas was the smith in 1871 and *his* son, also Thomas, is shown here in about 1900. The last smith, Leslie Jackson, retired in 1962 and the smithy became a garage, but the old mounting block was still there.

Hazel Grove had more blacksmiths than Bramhall because of the coaching trade. In 1858 there were at least five, one being a woman called Elizabeth Oldham. This smithy was in School Street and William Clarke, shown here, was the blacksmith in the 1930s.

Beside the smithy was the wheelwrights shop run by Thomas Seaton, seen here with his two dogs and William Clarke. In 1865 there were six wheelwrights in the directories. This century the skills of blacksmiths and wheelwrights have adapted to the motor vehicle, and Thomas Seaton was also a coach builder.

Timothy Walker's Removals. In the 1910 directory Timothy Walker appears as 'coal dealer and carrier' and lived at 47 Hazel Street, Hazel Grove. His removal van looks quite modern for the times, but was nevertheless pulled by horses from his stables in Vine Street.

It is said that the row of three storey gabled houses to the left of the Rising Sun was built in the hope of substantial compensation, expected when the houses would have to be demolished to make room for the Midland Railway in 1902. Unfortunately for the speculator, the line by-passed the cottages. They were used by the railway navvies when they worked in the village and are known locally as 'Navvy Mansions'.

Hazel Grove station was opened in 1857. After the Stockport viaduct had been built, an act of 1854 extended the railway from Stockport to Disley and Whaley Bridge, and to Buxton in 1863. The line was incorporated into the London & North Western Railway in 1866. There was a second station in Hazel Grove, on the Midland Railway. This was on the east side of the A6, beyond the viaduct.

Hazel Grove station as it was in July 1956, showing the overgrown loading dock and some of the cattle pens beyond. The site of the cattle pens is now used by the car park and bus stops are on the site of the old loading dock.

Wilfred Wood VC was one of Hazel Grove's war heroes. He earned his VC in 1918 for conspicuous bravery at Casa Vana in Italy. Armed only with a Lewis gun, he single-handedly secured the surrender of three officers and 300 men. In civilian life he was an engine driver. He and his wife are seen standing in front of the engine that was named in his honour on 18 July 1974.

Some teachers of the Methodist Sunday school in Hazel Grove on a rail trip to Aberystwyth - fare 7s 6d (37½p) return. This was taken outside Miss Clapperton's boarding house and shop in 1908. The men are Jim Smith and Jim Bennett and the ladies Jane Penney (later married to the photographer, Herbert Bennett), Martha Ellen Taylor (later Bennett), and Dora Annie Johnson (later Smith).

Bramhall Railway bridge. The station is to the right and was opened in 1845 when a line from Stockport to the Poynton collieries, via Cheadle Hulme and Bramhall, was built. In November of the same year the line was extended to Macclesfield. Later, to allow omnibuses to pass beneath, a new bridge was put in and the road was lowered under it. After heavy rain the dip in the road was liable to flood.

A tram of the Stockport and Hazel Grove Carriage and Tramway Company Ltd, which opened on 4 April 1889. Horse trams took over from the horse buses and ran between Hazel Grove and Manchester. The fare from Hazel Grove to Stockport was 3d and was collected by the conductor in instalments in a glass-fronted brass box, one penny being put into the box by the passenger at each fare stage. There was also a box for letters on the tram which the conductor posted at Stockport. This was not the first public service. In 1874 an enterprising landlord named Poulson had run a two-hourly wagonette service from the Bull's Head to the Warren Bulkeley Arms in Stockport. Two years later a Mr Dunn had a similar service running from the Red Lion seven times a day.

The new electric trams started in Manchester at the beginning of this century and replaced the horse trams. This is the Stockport Tramways tram shed, which was built at the rear of the Crown Inn, Hazel Grove (just north of the toll house). Stockport Borough took over the tramlines in 1901 when the lines were electrified. The first run was followed by a celebratory lunch inside the shed.

In Affectionate Remembrance

OF THE

Hazel Grove Horse Cars

Which Succumbed to an

ELECTRIC SHOCK

JULY 5th, 1905.

After many years of faithful Service.

"GONE, BUT NOT FORGOTTEN."

Copyright.

The end of the horse trams in 1905 was much lamented by the people of Hazel Grove. Somehow the new-fangled electric trams of Stockport Tramways were not the same, as this *In Memorium* card shows. The first motor omnibus service started in 1919 and in 1927-9 Mr Jack Sharpe ran a motor bus service every 15 minutes from Hazel Grove to Stockport.

Herbert Oldham ran his business, known as 'Cabby Oldham's', from this house on London Road. From early this century he met people from the trains and provided transport for weddings and funerals. Among his horse drawn vehicles were a victoria, a landau, a wagonette, a hansom cab and a trap. His stables were at 3 Lever Street, which became a garage when he changed to motor coaches.

Some folk took their outings in a horse drawn wagonette. Among the happy band here, in about 1914, are Frank Allen (back row left, without a hat) and his wife, and Albert Adshead (front left, in a cap).

This outing to Matlock in 1925 was organised by the Ladies' Bright Hour from the Wesleyan Methodist Church. They saved a penny a week to hire the charabanc from Royle's of Stockport. Mr Royle's son is driving, but is hidden by Mr J.T. Dean and his daughter Marion. The elderly gentleman to the rear is Mr Grundey. Travelling at 12 mph, they arrived at Matlock in time for dinner.

Surely this must be the most unusual of the transport photographs. Although the date is known to be 1903, and it was taken in Hazel Grove, the names of both driver and passenger are unknown - but what a lovely vehicle for fine sunny days!

One of the trucks used by Mirrlees, Bickerton & Day Limited during the First World War.

An accident during the Second World War on London Road, Hazel Grove. A lorry carrying supplies to the US Air Force Base at Woodford burst a front tyre and lost its load opposite the Red Lion. All the trams from Stockport had to turn back at Chapel Street and spectators making for the dog track near the Rising Sun had to walk. Happily the only casualty was the driver, who had a sprained ankle.

Five

Serving the Community

The ways in which various members of the community served their fellow men are revealed in this section, herbalist to hospital and pubs to police. The nature of the two villages influenced the number of public houses that opened. In Hazel Grove the demands of services for the coach routes led to the opening of many inns. Some, like the Red Lion, had large stables and their own smithy, as did the Grove Inn, whose smithy worked well into this century. Industry increased the population and the demand for drink, especially among those with thirsty jobs like navvies, miners and hatters. The Beer Act, which was designed to discourage the drinking of spirits, only added to the number of public houses. One disreputable beer house, the Blacksmith's Arms, was nicknamed the 'Blazing Rag', possibly a reflection of the socialist tendencies of its patrons. Eleven inns in Hazel Grove are described but there were at least twenty.

In Bramhall, under the restraining influence of the Davenports, there were far fewer. The earliest were the Leg of Mutton on Bramhall Green, which probably started as an ale house, and the Lamb Inn, which was on the edge of the manor on the Woodford boundary. The Jolly Sailor and the Victoria Hotel were only established in the late nineteenth century.

The shops in Hazel Grove developed piecemeal all along the line of the turnpike road through the village. Some were merely the front room of a cottage but early this century new ones were built. The development of the village of Bramhall in the last century encouraged a more compact layout of modern shops.

Local services included medical treatment, with both doctors and herbalists, and the workhouse hospital. Both villages had police stations and a tiny fire service existed in Bramhall.

The George and Dragon Inn, which stands at the site of one of the toll gates on London Road. In 1871 Ambrose Dransfield was landlord and toll house keeper until 1873. The licence of the inn is said to date from 1737. In the wall is a metal post with 'Manor and Barony of Stockport 1332' although it was put there in the last century. It marks the boundary of the borough.

The Grove Inn was opened in the early 1790s when it was named the Hazel Grove Inn. It may have dropped the 'Hazel' when the name of the village was changed from Bullock Smithy to Hazel Grove in 1836. Before the railway was built a coach service ran from the inn into Manchester, and the smithy behind it worked into this century.

The Anchor Inn was built before 1818 and was originally the Rope and Anchor. The annual village Celery Show, which included other vegetables and fruit, was held here in the latter half of the nineteenth century. The shows were followed by 'supper and a convivial evening'. Like many other pubs in the village, the Anchor brewed its own beer.

The Cock Inn (formerly the Game Cock). It was already an inn with a brew house when it was sold in 1817. From 1883 the Gosling family were landlords, and this group in the 1920s includes the landlord James Gosling in the light coloured coat. He also owned the first *Hazel Grove Gazette* and the Hazel Grove Picture Palace on Commercial Road.

The Grapes Hotel was licensed in 1795 when it was also a farm with cows, pigs and horses. Beyond it is the Three Tuns, where in 1855 the landlord reported his neighbour at The Grapes as causing 'a nuisance' by the 'offensive smell rising from its sewer' - then an open ditch running along the highroad past both inns and crossed by a plank!

The Horse and Jockey, Hazel Grove. The inn stands on London Road in the old township of Bosden. It started life as a beer house, when an act to discourage the sale of spirits in 1830 allowed a householder to sell beer from his house for an annual licence of only two guineas instead of ten guineas for a full licence. Many beer houses later became inns.

The horse tram to Stockport is outside J.H. Turner's grocery shop at the time of Edward VII's Coronation in 1901. This was the site of the Queen's Head Hotel which disappears from the records in 1825. It gave its name to the present Queens Road that replaced Engine Gennel, named after the horse gin that drove the first cotton mill in the Grove.

THE OLD FOX INN

An early photograph of the cottage that was the Fox and Goose Inn (or the Old Fox) which stood at the end of the row of cottages next to the Red Lion. Clementina Turner was the landlady from 1809 until it closed in 1838. Shady Lane (or the Shades) ran up behind it to join Button Lane, now Chester Road, by the present Conservative Club.

The Red Lion. The date stone reads 'Hazel Grove 1796' but was carved by Isaac Broadhurst in 1836 to emphasise the change of name of the village. The Fidlers were licensees from before 1754. They illegally leased the common land on Fidlers' Green, opposite, for five cottages, two loom shops, a smithy, and sundry pig cotes and shippens, until the Enclosure Act of 1811 stopped them. The inn became a posting house for the mail coach service and until recently had stables and a bowling green at the back.

This cottage near the Rising Sun, photographed in 1901, is said to be the Bullock Smithy Inn. The first inn is marked on Ogilby's map of 1675. This may be a renovation of the original house or a new building, but it is on the line of the old turnpike road.

The Rising Sun Inn stands at the junction of two turnpike roads, the Buxton, Chapel-en-le-Frith and Manchester (1724) and the Macclesfield Road (1762). The inn was a posting house and John Upton, the landlord between 1815 and 1860, was a 'veterinary surgeon and victualler'. The fountain was erected to commemorate Queen Victoria's Jubilee in 1887. Dr Moore used the surplus money from the Jubilee Fund to start a Sick-Nursing Association.

The original Jolly Sailor Inn, Bramhall, is in the centre of the photograph. It was licensed before 1872 and some say the licence of the Leg of Mutton Inn was transferred here. It was near to the present Jolly Sailor, which has a date stone 'AD 1895', and was possibly named after Admiral Salusbury Pryce Humphries of Bramall Hall. (See page 36)

The old Victoria Hotel was built some time before 1857, when James Hough was the landlord. This was the first of three Victoria Hotels and is shown here in 1900. It stood at the corner of Ack Lane and Bramhall Lane. Cash's Smithy can be seen on the left.

The Victoria Hotel, Bramhall.

The new Victoria Hotel was built in 1905 on the site of the original one. There were stables behind for the landlord, James Cottrill's, pony and trap. It was demolished in 1967 for the precinct. A third Victoria Hotel has been opened on Ack Lane, at the end of the shops. The Victoria was the only public house in the centre of the village and was very popular with the local farm workers.

This Co-operative store on London Road, Hazel Grove, was opened in 1860, although an attempt to open one had been made in 1852. Samuel Ridgeway, the first shop boy, is remembered for falling head first into a flour bin, but by 1905 he was general manager! Here the society is celebrating fifty years of trading on 30 July 1910. There was a gala, with the Hazel Grove Silver Band leading a procession of notables, and lorries laden with goods.

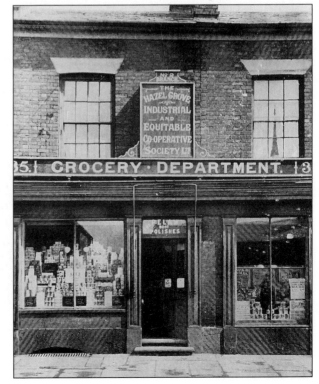

Such was the demand that other shops were opened, one at Norbury in 1890, this one in 1906 on the corner of Vernon Street, and another in 1910. Additions to the main shop included stables, a new butchery and bakery, offices, and an assembly hall. In 1877 the Co-op built eighty-eight cottages in three roads off Commercial Road, aptly named Hazel, Grove and Co-operative Streets.

The people owning these shops opposite the Civic Hall in 1910 had nicknames. There was 'Ducky Dean' who sold savoury ducks, a form of rissole; 'Wash Hallworth' the newsagent, whose parrot called out 'shop Wash' whenever anyone entered; and Dicky 'Pomp' the clogger in the cellar beneath, the proud owner of a piano who, if asked if he could play it, always replied 'No, only pomp-pomp'.

The shops on the left, on London Road near Lever Street, were owned by some other Grove characters. There was 'Chippy Bennet' with his fish and chip shop, 'Bum Grundey' the baker, and 'Tatty Hallworth' who made meat and potato pies.

J.T. Dean's shop on Hatherlow Lane, with Mrs Dean holding her baby. Before her marriage she was Annie Barlow, an orphan, who lived at Siddington Hall. She met John Dean when she was an apprentice at Grundey's, the bakers, of Grundey Street. They were married in 1887 and opened this shop, where she made pies and cakes for sale while he was a greengrocer.

These three shops stood on the corner of Chapel Street and London Road. The sweet shop of Miss Turnock on the corner was demolished to widen the road in 1910. The other two cottages were rebuilt by J.T. Dean as a greengrocers. Local butcher Harry Wilson has his horse and cart, and in the group are Billy Dump and his wife Alice.

Sarah Ann, wife of Jonah Thatcher, is standing at the door of her fresh fish shop in 1902. Her brother was Cyrus Webb. The fish shop had been in the Thatcher family for several generations and Jonah is said to have been related to Jonathan Thatcher, 'The Cheshire Farmer', who saddled his cow and rode it into Stockport market in 1784 in protest at the saddle tax on horses.

Robson's the grocers, on the corner of London Road and Queens Road, in the 1960s. This shows the shop shortly after it had been extended to include the premises of Oldham's the butchers. It was a family business and their friendly service included home deliveries - a luxury these days. In 1965/6 the premises were sold to Lennons, later Gateway, the first supermarket in the village.

Corrie's the greengrocers shop in Bramhall was built by W.L. Adkinson and is seen here c.
1896. Next door was the first post office in the village, run by Peter Rhodes in the front room of
his cottage. The board advertises insurance, annuities, money orders and the telegraph service.

By the 1930s Corrie's had expanded and two neighbouring private houses had been added to
the premises. Here is the shop at Christmas 1938 - would modern health controls allow such a
display today? The business was later taken over by another poulterer and greengrocer, Cyril
Swindells.

Mr and Mrs Peter Rhodes. He was the coachman for Mr Cyrus Slater of Ack Lane, but he developed Parkinson's disease and his employer helped him to open the first sub-post office in Bramhall. When his condition worsened his daughter, Miss Miriam Rhodes, took over as sub-postmistress when she was only 17.

BRAMHALL POST OFFICE.

In 1895 Peter Rhodes moved his stationery shop and post office to the corner of Lumb Lane. The sorting office was in the cellar beneath and letters from the post box fell straight there down a chute. A new post office on Maple Road was opened in 1953 and it was from here that the last Rhodes, Miriam's brother Cephas, retired as sub-postmaster in 1962 at the age of 75.

Cecil Wood's on Lever Street. In about 1860 James Wood of Hazel Grove, a cotton manufacturer, took advantage of a slump in trade to earn money from his hobby. He began to sell his herbal remedies and advice with great success. But it was his third son, Cecil, who opened the firm in 1867. In the 1870s, after his father's death, he moved into his father's cottage here, and soon extended his premises into the next two cottages.

The photograph of Cecil Wood, herbalist, appears on his advertising postcard, c. 1902. His reps travelled as far as Buxton and Blackpool to sell his remedies, the flu powders being especially popular. He held surgeries and published booklets on healthy living, recommending high fibre, avoiding fatty foods and eating tomatoes and bananas. He died in the 1920s but it was competition from the NHS that closed the firm in 1966.

More orthodox medicine was practised by the two Drs Moore, 'Old Tom' and 'Young Tom', father and son, seen here in 1905. They worked from their home, Moseley House, now the site of the present health centre, and made their visits in a pony and trap. Both were greatly loved and respected. The baby is 'Young Tom's' son. 'Old Tom' was the Medical Officer of Health for Hazel Grove and doctor to the Stockport Union.

The sanatorium of Stepping Hill Hospital. The hospital was originally built as a workhouse hospital and was part of the Stockport Union. It was opened on 7 December 1905 at a cost of some £5,000. There were four blocks, each with three wards. In 1934, on the abolition of the Boards of Guardians, it was transferred to Stockport Corporation and was named Stepping Hill Hospital. It is now a NHS hospital.

Hazel Grove Police Station was built some time before 1858. One Saturday night in 1905 there was a riot because the local easy-going sergeant was replaced by new over-zealous officers who arrested a local carter for being 'drunk in charge'. Bricks were thrown through the police station windows and it was 3 a.m. before order was restored. A crowd gathered again the next evening but were persuaded to go home by John Adshead and Superintendent McHail, and all charges were dropped.

The police cottage, or 'Cheshire Constabulary', at Pownall Green. The original police station had been in a timber framed cottage on Bramhall Green, and William Gatley was the policeman in 1885. At the beginning of this century the police station was moved into the right hand part of this house on Bramhall Lane South.

These Bramhall firemen, c. 1900, have an early horse drawn fire engine and are busy training with their webbing hose. The engine was kept in a shed on Lumb Lane. Mr Pridgeon, the ironmonger, had some horses which he lent if they were free at the time of a fire. The firemen were volunteers and included John Corrie, Harry Leah, Walter Seed and Mr Whitehead.

The greatest service is to give one's life and the War Memorial bears witness to those in Hazel Grove who fell in the two World Wars. It stands in the gardens on London Road on land given by Major Peter Pierce JP of Poynton and the Wesleyan Primitive Methodist Church. The memorial was unveiled on Sunday 11 November 1923.

Six

Industry

It was the established transport system and to a lesser extent streams for water-power that encouraged industrial development in Hazel Grove. Cottage industry was part of the life of a farmer or smallholder and many homes in both Hazel Grove and Bramhall made space for a handloom. Silk was hand woven throughout the area from the eighteenth century. Most of the thrown silk came from the mills in Macclesfield, although in the nineteenth century silk mills for throwing and manufacturing ribbons and trimmings opened in Hazel Grove.

A Thomas Moseley was putting out the materials for checks and fustian to local handloom weavers by 1754, and muslin and calico in 1794. Cotton spinning was introduced by Henry Marsland, who started in Hazel Grove in 1761 with a weaving shed and a cotton factory, using spinning frames powered by a horse gin. This gave its name to Engine Gennel. In 1783 he moved to the Park Mills, Stockport, and lived at Woodbank Hall. In 1836 David Moseley built the water-powered Wellington Mill and workers' houses in the Bosden Valley in Hazel Grove. Cotton spinning and weaving continued in the various mills that opened. Hatting was another industry, both in the factory and the home. In Hazel Grove 'Peggy' Johnson had a large wood yard where he made peggies for doing the weekly wash - and Anah Burns in Vine street provided the tubs. Engineering too became an important industry, from the work of the early navvies who built the railways, to present day firms like Mirrlees and Philips.

This photograph, taken in about 1918, shows Mrs Sarah Ann Ridgeway, a silk weaver, with her niece Alice Dennerly, then aged 7, on Bramhall Moor Lane. Alice could remember the clacking of the shuttles on the loom, which was referred to locally as 'poverty knocking' because it was so poorly paid.

Children did not weave but they were expected to help by winding silk onto the perns, or spools, which went into the shuttles. This little girl is using a wheel similar to a spinning wheel, and a tray of wound perns can be seen at her feet. The children also had to do the jobs about the house that might roughen the weavers' hands and cause snags in the fine silk.

90

Edna Hammond working at her loom early this century. Her earnings went towards supporting three of her motherless nieces who lived with her. She was the owner of the loom shop, shown below, until she died in 1931, by which time there were few weavers left. Betty Penney, of No. 33 Chester Road, is reputed to be the last to weave her red silk in the village.

At the back of No. 41 Hatherlow Lane was a loom shop with space for four looms. The light from the large windows and whitewashed walls was excellent for the very fine work. Spare loom space was rented to other weavers. Silk loom shops had their entrances within the house so that dust from outside could not damage the delicate silk. Hazel Grove still has a number of converted loom shops behind the cottages.

The parade is passing two other cottages in Hatherlow Lane, Nos 23 and 25, which had their loom shops within the house itself. Many houses were custom-built for the trade. The weaving rooms had closed square windows while the living rooms had fashionable sash windows. Here some of the upstairs and downstairs rooms were used for weaving.

This loom shed is at the back of another cottage in Hatherlow Lane. During a slump in trade in 1826 nearly 450 weavers out of a total of 562 were unemployed in Hazel Grove, and 32 years later there were 800 looms reported idle in the Grove.

This loom shop, behind No. 80 London Road, was demolished in the 1980s when land was needed for the car park for the new Co-operative store. It stood in the southern corner of the car park and could house several looms. The remains of one were still inside it.

This terrace of cottages in Spring Gardens, built in 1838, shows another type of loom shop where the cellars were used for weaving. The ground floor was entered up a few steps, so that daylight was let into the workshops below. Here the modern pavement is up to the house fronts, hiding the original windows. In this short street there were thirty-one silk weavers in the 1871 census.

John Street was custom-built for a weaving community. At the east end of the terrace was No. 7, shown here, which from the front appeared to be a large residential cottage with a date stone of 1896, fashionable sashed windows and carved barge boards to the gable.

But the rear of No. 7 tells a different story. The upper rooms have square weaving windows and built onto the back of the house is a large loom shop. The chimney served an iron stove, usually the only heating in a shed, since silk wove better in cool damp air. The dampness, which was said to produce a bloom on the cloth, came from a trodden earth floor.

The backs of the other houses, Nos 3 and 5 in John Street, have the large square windows in the upper storey which show that these rooms were used for weaving. The living quarters were at the front of the cottages. The photographs were taken just before the whole road was demolished in the 1970s.

This house, on the corner of John Street and Mount Pleasant, had a warping attic which supplied the warps for the local weavers. Some of the warps from Macclesfield came already prepared, like a thick rope. In the 1920s one lady in Hazel Grove who specialised in putting the warps onto the looms charged 2s 6d ($12\frac{1}{2}$p) for her day's work.

Far prettier are these cottages in Benja Fold, Bramhall. They are cruck framed and the nearer one, the thatched cottage, was the home of the Leah family. In 1851 Ann Leah and Edward Bennet were handloom silk weavers. An outshut built on the gable end of the cottage was used as a loom shop The pump on the left provided water for a wide area. The Fold was called after an eighteenth century owner of the land, Benjamin Birchenough. Peter Pownall, who owned it later and was a Unitarian, refused the Methodists' request to have the use of his barn as a chapel. This century, to save the Fold from demolition, Sir Thomas Rowbotham bought it. Today the cottages are owner occupied.

ROBINS LANE, BRAMHALL (No. 2.)

These cottages stood on the corner of Robins Lane, on Pownall Green in Bramhall, and were lived in by silk weavers. An outshut loom shop can be seen at the far end. In the 1841 census twenty-one silk weavers are recorded on the Green. The cottages were damaged by a bomb in the Second World War and demolished for road widening in the 1950s.

Cash's cottages in 1895. The two cruck framed, thatched cottages stood at the end of Syddal Houses with the gable end facing down Bramhall Lane South. According to the 1871 census the nearer cottage was lived in by John Redfern, a silk weaver, and his wife and six children. He is seen standing in the doorway. The Cash family, who lived next door in 1892, were blacksmiths.

The Bull's Head Inn in Hazel Grove. On the corner opposite was Torkington House, originally the site of Gaskell's Silk Mill. This is said to be the first mill in Hazel Grove, where silk throwing and spinning took place in the upper rooms. In 1813 a Samuel Gaskell appears in directories as a check (probably muslin) manufacturer. Behind the Bull's Head was the bowling green, a popular feature in many Hazel Grove pubs.

Bate Hall Mill, on the A6, was owned in 1858 by Joel Grundy and William Etchells. The latter was a silk manufacturer and sold silk goods to the hatting trade, bringing his silk from Macclesfield on a handcart. At one time Samuel Penney rented a winding room and a loom shop on the premises. In 1880 Bate Hall came up for auction and was purchased by the newly formed Hazel Grove Co-operative Society.

Oak Street Mill, Hazel Grove, was built by Samuel Fidler and in 1868 was a steam driven silk mill. From 1871-91 John Unwin was a heald manufacturer and silk doubler here. In 1900 it was a hatworks under Messrs Bardsley, Gibson & Taylor. R.J. Fletcher followed, but by 1910 sewing cotton was manufactured there by Briggs & Armstrong. Beyond Oak Street was Enoch ('Peggy') Johnson's, a wood turning mill.

Vine Street Silk Mill with 'Vine Cottage' in the foreground. Built sometime in the 1850s, it was owned by the Heys family, muslin manufacturers since 1794. By 1857 the mill was processing silk. After the 1870s John Robert Webb moved from the Albion Mill to Vine Street and made silk trimmings. The garden wall was the end of Vine Street until the house and mill were demolished in 1938. The little girls are John's grandchildren, the daughters of his son Cyrus Webb.

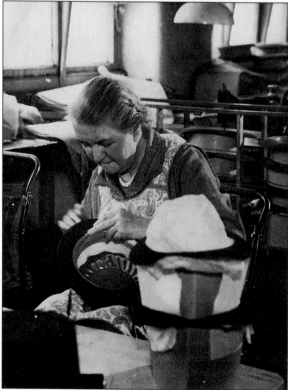

Cyrus Webb was also a silk manufacturer, specialising in ribbons, tassels and leather bands for the hatting industry. An inventor, in 1915 he patented a machine to weave silk ribbons with spaces in the weave to make them into tiny bows more easily. Later he developed the machine in the photograph, which actually tied the bows, with patents in many foreign countries. He traded with America and Russia.

Miss Elsie Preston trimming hats at Christy's after the last war. She was one of the orphaned nieces of Miss Hammond, the silk weaver. In the Grove many women did 'out-work', when hats were delivered to their homes in black bags. They trimmed them by putting linings, bands and the tiny silk bows inside the hats, and ribbons round the outside. The paper tissues were to protect the hats.

Samuel Penney, born in 1851, was the son of a silk weaver and had a silk trimmings works at the Bate Mill. Later he started a firm making the paper tissues for packing hats, with a workshop off Commercial Road. He was a member of the Wesleyan Church, and using only tonic solfa he taught singing and wrote hymns, often played by the Hazel Grove Band which he loved to conduct. He also wrote about the village's history. He died in 1932.

Green Mount was the home of Thomas Rowbotham, hat manufacturer at Albion Mill. Here he and his wife Hannah reared their large family of thirteen children. They kept a cow and compelled their children to drink the milk. In 1882 Thomas patented his invention for curling the brims of bowler hats. After the closure of the firm in 1887 due to money problems, the family had to move, but Thomas continued with his inventions, including one for putting boot polish into tins, until his death in 1898.

The Albion Mill in Commercial Road was built around 1847 as a silk mill, and is seen here in 1982 before it was demolished for Kwik Save. The first owner was J.R. Webb, then in 1864 Messrs Axon, Grundy and Rowbotham moved there from their Bosden Works (originally Turner's glue works and later a laundry). By 1907 Abijah Barton and Sons were there making cotton wadding, in great demand during the First World War, when it was known as 'Badger Barton's'.

The Hazel Grove Mill at the north end of the village. It was a silk mill in 1850 but by 1870 Lawrence Arden had extended it to manufacture sewing and crochet cotton. He joined the newly formed English Sewing Cotton Company in 1898 and the mill became a box-making and printing works. One of the labels they printed was for Dewhurst's Sylko. The public weighbridge was by the mill, and behind there was a reservoir. The mill was demolished in 1955.

The Wellington Cotton Mill was at the bottom of Bosden Fold Road. Built in 1836 for David Moseley by Mr Fletcher, a local builder, by 1844 it was owned by John Cooper, of Poise House. Originally water-powered, it was one of the first mills to have steam-powered looms and by 1866 was supplying gas to the village. By 1888 it had been taken over by the Hollin's Mill Co. Over 400 Grovers worked there from 6 a.m. till 5.30 p.m. and, until the 1920s, children under 12 were employed as 'part-timers', working half a day.

Fire was an ever-present danger in cotton mills and this fire in 1964 completely destroyed the old Wellington Mill. Hollins looked after their employees well, providing a recreation centre and tea parties and even holding wedding receptions for them. In 1937 Hollins closed the mill and transferred many of the hands to their other mill in Marple. Later the building was occupied by different firms, including a textile printing works.

The 'Clock Tower' at Norbury Colliery, which housed the winding gear, was built in about 1840, adjacent to the colliery offices. The land belonged to Col Thomas Peter Legh of Lyme Park who appointed Nathaniel Wright in 1789 to run the mine and installed two steam engines in 1799. Before that a Newcomen engine had been used to drain the mine. In 1841 there were 129 miners employed, many from Hazel Grove. The colliery closed in April 1892. The building was converted to a dwelling house in 1960.

One of the oldest companies in the area is Mirrlees Blackstone, who can trace their origin back to 1840. They arrived in Hazel Grove in 1908 when the Mirrlees Watson Company of Glasgow wanted to expand its production of diesel engines. They built a factory on Bramhall Moor Lane and the photograph shows this as it was during the First World War, when the company name was Mirrlees, Bickerton & Day Ltd.

104

The factory played an important role during the war years, not only producing their standard range of diesel engines but also a special type of engine for installation in tanks. This is one of the tanks built by the Mirrlees Watson Co. Ltd and fitted with a Mirrlees, Bickerton & Day's engine, made in Hazel Grove. The engine proved to be most successful and a large number of them were made. The tanks were first used in 1916 and helped to revolutionise ideas in warfare.

Part of the tool room at Mirrlees, Bickerton & Day during the First World War. To cope with the increased demand for diesel engines the factory was expanded and it was necessary to take on a large number of extra workers. Almost all of these were women, the army having absorbed so many of the men.

The furniture factory on School Street, Hazel Grove, which helped to make Mosquito aircraft during the Second World War. In 1956 the factory was bought by GEC who used it for microwave and power semiconductor production.

Part of the production line making semiconductors at the School Street factory of GEC. In 1959 the factory employed 700 people, half of whom were women working in the main assembly shop. By 1970 the business was being run by Mullard, owned by Philips, who transferred production to a new site on Bramhall Moor Lane.

Seven

Celebrations

Originally many of the celebrations or festivals in a community were associated with the church and Hazel Grove has a long history of such events, including the Wakes. In the north the Wakes Week holiday continued well into this century. Originally the vigil or 'wake' was kept in the church on the eve of the patron saint. Gradually the Wakes became an excuse for secular revelry. The Norbury (later Bullock Smithy) Wakes started on the second Sunday in August and lasted for several days, the whole village coming to a standstill. There was always a fair and competitions, with trials of strength, followed by dancing every evening.

The new churches of the nineteenth century exerted their influence over the style of celebrations, which gradually became more restrained. There were many church processions through the village and the band was always ready to lead the way. A more recent innovation has been the annual carnival procession. The greatest celebration of all was in 1836 when the name of the village was changed from Bullock Smithy to Hazel Grove in an attempt to improve its reputation. In this century the centenary was celebrated in 1936, and the 150th in 1986 - the last a more modest affair.

By contrast the mainly farming community of Bramhall, centred round the manor house, had fewer opportunities for revelry and celebrations were of a more decorous nature under the watchful eyes of the Davenports, although both Bramhall and Hazel Grove celebrated the coronations and anniversaries of royalty.

The Hazel Grove Band, formed around the 1830s, was also known as the Brass, and later the Silver, Band. It was an important part of village life for over a hundred years. Here they can be seen leading Norbury Church Sunday School scholars in a procession of witness. Their German style of helmet was changed to a flat cap during the First World War.

Hazel Grove Brass Band.

OFFICIAL GUIDE AND PROGRAMME

OF ARRANGEMENTS OF THE

GRAND BAZAAR,

TO BE HELD IN THE

MECHANICS' - INSTITUTE,

HAZEL GROVE,

On Thursday, Friday, and Saturday,

JULY 19th, 20th, & 21st, 1894,

IN AID OF THE HAZEL GROVE BRASS BAND

NEW INSTRUMENT FUND.

PRICES OF ADMISSION:

FAMILY TICKET, to Admit Two together of one family - 2s. 6d.
SEASON TICKET, to Admit One all days (not transferable) - 1s. 6d.
THURSDAY, ALL DAY - - - - - 1s.
FRIDAY, to Six o'clock - 1s. After Six o'clock - 6d.
SATURDAY, ALL DAY - - - - - 6d.

Anyone dissatisfied with these charges will be allowed to pay again when leaving the Bazaar.

PROGRAMMES THREEPENCE EACH.

The Grand Bazaar in July 1894. It had been decided in 1882 that the band, rather than members, should own the instruments, and 'five of Messrs Besson & Co's famous Electroplated Patent Prototype Instruments' had already been bought. The bazaar was to raise money to buy more instruments for them. Each day there was an opening ceremony, performed on the Saturday by Mrs Nevill of Bramall Hall.

The band in the 1930s. They practised in a room at the rear of the Bird in Hand Inn. Every Christmas Eve, at midnight, they started playing seasonal music on the forecourt where the crowds joined in the carols, bringing the traffic to a halt. Then they went, still playing lustily, all round the village, all night. The awakened sleepers invariably rewarded them with refreshments, both food and drink - not without affecting the playing!

This procession, passing the Civic Hall, is to celebrate the Floral Fête in Hazel Grove early this century. The young girls have flowers in their hair, and from the crowd lining the route it seems that most of the village is there to watch them. Behind the hoarding the Primitive Methodist Church is visible, and on the wall at the right a sign points the way to the railway station.

The people of Hazel Grove loved a procession and in 1936 the opportunity to celebrate the centenary of the renaming of the village was too good a chance to miss. The new name of Hazel Grove had been made official on Saturday 26 September 1836, when there was a grand procession to record the 'annihilation of the name of Bullock Smithy'. The streets were decorated with flags and flowers and a reputed '5,000 persons were present'. Then there were tea parties for the children and free beer for others! Here, among the parade a hundred years later, is the Congregational Sunday school with their huge banner held aloft. The traffic was held up as they marched along the tramlines and anyone not already in the procession gathered to watch.

Outside the Red Lion preparations are being made for the centenary parade. The stage coach was once used in the village and the passengers are in costume. The young girl standing in the centre is Ann Gosling, on her right is Annie Rowbotham, and on her left Nellie Jones.

Fifty years later, on 27 September 1986, the 150 years celebration parade took place. Here are some members of the Hazel Grove Local History Group: from left to right, in the foreground, Tom and Hilda Gosling, behind, Tony Gosling, and Heather and Angus Coutie. The 'banner' is a copy of the 'coat of arms' (see page 127). They are followed by the Hazel Grove Musical Festival Society with Eric Adshead holding their banner.

The annual Bullock Smithy Wakes were originally held on Brewer's Green and later on Back o'th Barn field at Old Fold Farm, but here they are on land behind the Albion Mill. The mill was extended sometime after 1907 and a crane can be seen in the back of the picture. Bull baiting and cockfighting were usual in the last century but this happy crowd are content with poking harmless fun at the expense of the Hazel Grove Band.

The Hazel Grove Twins were Sam Clough and James Rowbotham and were not related. With black faces and doleful expressions they used to entertain at concert parties. Around 1919 they started to collect money for charity - you had to pay them if you could not make them laugh. At the Stockport Carnival in 1945 they raised £101 7s 10d, and by 1946 they had raised a total of nearly £10,000.

Hazel Grove has had an annual Carnival procession since the last war. Here Tom Gosling is preparing one of the great cart horses to pull a float in the early 1950s.

This was taken from the back of a tram on the day the first old age pensions were paid in Hazel Grove. Jimmy Holt ('Tinker Jimmy') was the first to receive his single man's allowance of 5s (25p). Outside the old post office the crowd sang *Praise God From Whom All Blessings Flow*. Pensions for people over 70 were introduced in 1908 by Lloyd George, and in 1928 the qualifying age was lowered to 65 years.

Coronation Day, Bramhall,
26th June, 1902.

ADMIT

Margaret Higgins

to Tea in the Village Hall, at 3 o'clock p.m.,
and to Refreshments at 8 p.m.

After Tea, each child will receive a Bag of Sweets
and an Orange, kindly provided by Mrs. Preston.

This Ticket must be shown at 1-15 p.m. before the Procession
in order to obtain the Medal or Brooch, given by Mr. Preston.

It Must also be shown on entering the Village Hall to Tea

For the coronation of Edward VII on 26 June 1902, Bramhall had a procession and medals or brooches were distributed to the holders of these tickets. They were also entitled to tea in the Village Hall, each child receiving an orange and a bag of sweets afterwards, and to refreshments in the evening. Mr and Mrs Preston provided all the gifts. Margaret Higgins kept this ticket among her souvenirs.

In 1937 Bramhall celebrated the coronation of George VI. Viewed from the railway bridge, the procession is passing Benja Fold. On the left can be seen the lay-by of sets outside the railway station where, around 1914, the cabs of Mr John Wright Hodgson, 'carriage proprietor', of Moss Lane used to meet passengers from the trains. He had eight horses and used black ones for funerals and brown for weddings.

In Hazel Grove they nominated their own queen for the coronation festivities of George VI in 1937. Dorothy Middleton sits proudly on her float, having been crowned by Mrs Dean. She and her lady-in-waiting are on Gresty's field, ready for the procession to start.

On 27 June 1977 the Queen, with Prince Philip, arrived at the refurbished Hazel Grove station to begin their visit to the north west, in celebration of her Silver Jubilee. She drove through the village, greeted by Grovers lining the streets, then along the A6 to Manchester for a very long day of engagements.

Hatherlow Lane in 1945, decorated with bunting and flags to celebrate the end of the Second World War. Like many other roads they had a street party.

In spite of the photographs above, the weather was not always kind for processions, as can be seen here. Umbrellas shield the dainty dresses of the girls described as from 'the Church School', presumably Norbury School. No doubt the Hazel Grove Band was drenched as well.

Eight
Recreation

All work and no play was not part of the philosophy of the people of Hazel Grove and Bramhall, and this section aims to show just a small sample of the many recreational activities in which they indulged. The recreation ground in Hazel Grove was opened in 1893 to commemorate the wedding of the Duke of York and Princess Mary of Teck, and used for many public celebrations. Both villages were keenly interested in sport with cricket and football teams and later tennis and golf. More recently the Bullock Smithy hike preserves the old name of the village, a real challenge at 56 miles, while somewhat less demanding were the agricultural shows and the humble pigeon fanciers' and celery growers' competitions. Bramhall had an indoor and open air swimming pool.

Exercise for the mind was not forgotten and music has always been a feature of both villages. This century saw the Hazel Grove Music Festival, which is still thriving today, and choirs were an integral part of church life, with members joining other choirs too. Sam Penney wrote hymns for the choirs in Hazel Grove and the band paraded the village playing some of them. More recently music of a different sort has been heard in Bramhall, where Scottish dancing flourishes.

For recreation of a gentler sort there were lectures to attend in the Mechanics Institute in Hazel Grove which had a library, a news room and a billiards room, and many different societies in both villages. Less testing to the mind were the two picture palaces in Hazel Grove and another in Bramhall. Amateur dramatics flourished and some of the cast of Coronation Street stretched their wings at the Marcliffe Cinema on Macclesfield Road, which was also a repertory theatre.

Bramall Park Golf Club, with some early members outside their pavilion. On 8 October 1894 forty men met at Benjamin Ashwell's house to discuss the construction of a golf course in Bramhall. Only five weeks later, after they had formed a club and laid out a rough nine-hole course on land off Ravenoak Road, the first round was played - what an achievement! The present clubhouse on Manor Road was built in 1923.

Hazel Grove Cricketers, 1883. This splendid group of gentlemen used to play their cricket on a field behind the Rising Sun Hotel. Back row, left to right: Sam Williamson (non-player), John Kellit, Billy Mather (umpire), Martin Clough, Jack Fletcher, Sam Burns. Middle row: George Hallam (secretary), Anah Burns, Robert Penney, Sam Hallworth, Bill Penney. Front row: J. Roberts, Jim Kellit, J. Higinbotham.

One of the early cricket teams in Hazel Grove was made up entirely of butchers from the village, and was known simply as 'The Cricketing Butchers'. This photograph of them was taken in about 1905. Six of them worked for the Co-op but some others, such as Bill Oldham, had their own shops.

Wesley Park, by the Midland Railway line, was the home of the Hazel Grove Wesleyan Cricket Club, formed in 1906. Two of the original members of that club, Mr F. Bennett and Mr S. Jackson, were present at a ceremony in April 1937 when this new pavilion was formally opened prior to the first match of the season against Chapel-en-le-Frith.

Hazel Grove Football Club in 1924, the year they won the cup. Front row, left to right: Johnson, Hopkinson, Jones, Dr Tom Moore, Noland, Yewdale and Grundy. Centre row: Mr J.A. Daniels, Mr Hadfield, Bracewell, Daniels, Johnson, Mr R. Brown, Mr Billy Wooding, Broome, Poole, Hill, Ridgway. Back row: Mr Adshead, Mr John Wooding, Mr Johnson, Mr Bill Broome, Mr Downs, Mr Bowdell, Mr Cooke.

Bramhall Football Club in the 1890s. The club started in 1886 due largely to Dr W.E. Bond, the first village doctor, who captained the original team and was club secretary and sole selector! The team played at Lumb Farm and around 1900 it included Joe Ford and A. Corrie. The Bramhall Cricket Club was also established in 1886, playing on a field adjacent to what is now Queensgate. The football and cricket clubs later became part of the Queensgate Sports Club.

Members of the Bramhall Lane Lawn Tennis Club after their club championship in 1957. The club started in 1907 with twenty-eight members and two grass courts in a field off Bramhall Lane. It was not until 1924 that the club was officially named. In 1927 the present, much larger, site was acquired. Brenda Newport, at the far left of the photograph, became the first lady president of the club in 1993.

The old name for Hazel Grove is commemorated each year in the Bullock Smithy Hike, organised since 1976 by the 3rd Hazel Grove Scouts, which starts and finishes in Hazel Grove. It takes place in early September over a 56 mile course among the hills of the Peak District and involves 11,000 feet of climbing. The race is traditionally started by striking a smith's anvil, and the photograph shows the start in 1977.

Bramhall Show, 1927. The show originated from a meeting of nine men on 29 October 1888 in the billiard room of Mr T.A. Addyman's house, Hillbrook Grange. They decided to set up the Bramhall and Woodford Horticultural Society with Mr Charles Nevill as president and Mr Addyman as chairman, and to organise an annual Bramhall Show. The first of these was held on 24 August 1889 in a tent in a field off Ack Lane, but for the next thirty years they were held in the grounds of Bramall Hall. There were initially three sections to the competitive events - one for gentlemen gardeners, one for cottagers living within three miles of Bramhall station and a third for farm and dairy produce within a five mile radius. Later the show was extended to include agricultural entries. The society, now known as the Bramhall, Cheadle Hulme & Woodford Agricultural & Horticultural Society, celebrated their centenary in 1988 and, after some wartime gaps, staged the 100th show in 1995.

Mr J. Worsley Harrop, who founded the Hazel Grove Musical Festival in 1921. He was well known in the area for his organ recitals, and a choir master and teacher. He was the conductor of the Hazel Grove Male Voice Choir for many years and choir master at Hazel Grove Methodist Church from 1908 until his death in 1944. Following the Second World War the festival resumed under the direction of Elsie Harrop, Worsley's younger sister.

The Ladybrook Ladies Choir returning from their tour of Canada in 1939. The choir was formed in 1928 by Elsie Harrop, who conducted it until her death in 1960. She combined the Hazel Grove Council School's Girls Choir with the Bramhall Methodist Church Choir to form the Ladybrook Ladies Choir, named after the stream that runs between Hazel Grove and Bramhall. They were later renamed the Ladybrook Singers and from 1969, the Hazel Grove Ladybrook Singers.

The cast in a production of *HMS Pinafore* performed at Norbury School in 1949. Jim Fearnley is centre back, wearing a cocked hat. His sister Ethel is in the front row, third from the right, with Mrs Friell - owner of the photograph - fifth from the left in the second row.

Scottish dancing has been a popular activity in the area for many years. The Bramhall Branch of the Royal Scottish Country Dance Society was formed in 1963. Some of its members are shown here dancing in Stockport Town Hall during the 1970s where they were taking part in an annual festival organised by the Goyt Valley Scottish Country Dance Club.

Bramhall Swimming Pool in the late 1930s. This was built about 1930 by Mr Walter Warren Stansby who lived in a house on the hill overlooking the site on Bramhall Park Road. There was initially a single outdoor pool but over a period of time he added a children's paddling pool and a cafe, then put a roof over the paddling pool and deepened it to form an indoor pool and added a new outdoor paddling pool. The baths were built on land adjacent to the Bramhall Park Tennis Club that Mr Stansby founded in 1926, using an ex-army guard hut from the First World War as the first club house. By the late 1960s the baths were no longer a going concern and in 1971 the tennis club acquired part of the land and used it to create a car park. Much of the rest of the land was sold for housing.

The Hazel Grove Picture Palace on Commercial Road was opened in 1913, but known locally as the 'Cosy Grove'. The pensioners have just seen George VI's Coronation. In the 1930s the owners, Mr and Mrs Hall, used to give 600 children a Boxing Day film show and Mr J.E. Gosling, who built the cinema, was Santa Claus. The cinema was closed in 1960 and the PO sorting office was built on the site. A second cinema, the Marcliffe on Macclesfield Road, opened in 1939.

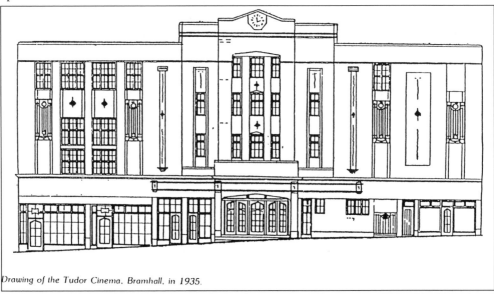

Drawing of the Tudor Cinema, Bramhall, in 1935.

A drawing of the Tudor Cinema, Bramhall. This stood on the corner of Woodford Road and Meadway and opened on 31 March 1935. Inside the stained oak panelling and massive oak pillars gave it a Tudor feeling, enhanced by portraits of Henry VIII and his six wives. It eventually closed in 1958 and was demolished in 1961.

An old Grover, Robert Daniels, used to entertain people with stories about the alleged naivety of his neighbours by reciting the 'poem' below. One of his friends then designed a special coat of arms for the village, which appears in the centenary procession shown on page 111. This was perpetuated on tea services, remains of which still exist and are much prized by their owners.

PEGG YUM TUBUM   NON SMALLPOXO
CLICKIN TOADUM WIREUM NETTUM

Hazel Grove and its Funny Folk

'The other day', said Higgins,' I
Was talking to a cove:
A funny sort of bloke he was,
Who came from Hazel Grove.

He said as how the folks theer had
Some very funny ways:
They did some funny things, and said
Some very funny says.

They fairly took the cake for being
Cleanest of the clean:
In fact they were the cleanest folk
He said he'd ever seen.

They polish up the furniture,
The metal and the brass,
Till all the blessed house looks like
A blooming looking-glass.

They clean the bricks outside the door,
And stone the flags as well.
In fact the folks have gone clean daft
On cleaning you can tell.

For when t' tram lines were laid
At least I've heard it said,
The folks came out and polished them
With brushes and black lead.

When Bullock Smithy Band were playing
Once in Brammer Lane,
A chap he put his pig on t'wall,
To listen to the strain.

And when the smallpox were very bad
In places far and near,
The Hazel Grovers said as how
They wouldner have it there.

And so in all the streets and roads,
At t' toll bar and about
They put some wire netting up,
To keep the smallpox out.

And once when Bullock Smithy Band
Were practising at neet,
A chap came in and said it sounded
Lovely in the street.

He said as how the music was
Both beautiful and clear;
So they all put down their instruments,
And went outside to hear.'

Acknowledgements

This book would not have been possible without the co-operation of my friends and the many people in Hazel Grove and Bramhall who have helped with my research, or generously lent their photographs, during the last twenty odd years that I have worked on local history. Many of the older folk helped me in another way, by patiently talking about times gone by. Although there are too many to mention all of them by name, I would like in particular to express my thanks to Jessie Burlace, Alice Daniels, Patty Dawson, Miss Dean, Miss A. Dennerley, Peter Friell, Tom and Tony Gosling, Fred Moss, Mr G. Parrott, Miss Pearson, Phyllis Pott, Elsie Preston, Fred Ridgway, Wendy Robinson, Mrs Sankey, Mrs Thornley, Sylvia Torkington, Mrs E. Warren and Cyrus Webb. Sadly some are no longer with us, but their memories live on.

More recently I have been amazed at the co-operation I have received from local firms, members of sports clubs, youth organisations, music societies and many others who have helped to fill in the gaps I had in my collection. In particular I am grateful for the help I have received from John Allen, Peter Babbage, Pauline Barker, Mrs Baskerville, Mac and Joan Birnie, Tom Bowden, Frank Brooks, Ken Daniels, Mr G. Dicken of Philips Semiconductors, Anne Hearle, Elizabeth Hessey, Miss M. Miller, Brenda Newport, Judy Oldroyd, Sandra Paterson, Gordon and Joyce Robson, Michael Smith, Mr K.W. Stansby, and Peter Wood of Mirrlees Blackstone Ltd.

I must also acknowledge my debt to the local historians whose publications have been useful in compiling my captions. In particular, I have learnt much from the writings of Barbara Dean, who is a widely recognised authority on Bramhall; Class 4W (1981) and their teacher Glynis Wilsdon at Pownall Green Junior School with their *Memories of Bramhall*; the late Frank Mitchell, who also gave me some of his collection of photographs; and, from earlier times, the writings of R.J. Fletcher and Sam Penney.

It gives me great pleasure to express my thanks to the staff of the Stockport Local Heritage Library, particularly David Reid and Ros Lathbury, who for many years have encouraged and helped me in recording the results of my research for future generations.

Last, but by no means least, I wish to thank my husband, Angus, because without his never ending patience, discipline and constructive help this book would never have been produced.